# WORKBOOK

# WORKBOOK

## A Simple Guide for
## Writing Educational Theses and Dissertations

Ojoma Edeh Herr

authorHOUSE®

*AuthorHouse™*
*1663 Liberty Drive*
*Bloomington, IN 47403*
*www.authorhouse.com*
*Phone: 1-800-839-8640*

*First published by AuthorHouse    09/12/2011*

*ISBN: 978-1-4634-8767-6 (sc)*
*ISBN: 978-1-4634-8766-9 (ebk)*

*Library of Congress Control Number: 2011915233*

*Printed in the United States of America*

*Any people depicted in stock imagery provided by Thinkstock are models, and such images are being used for illustrative purposes only.*
*Certain stock imagery © Thinkstock.*

*This book is printed on acid-free paper.*

# DEDICATION

I would like to thank my husband, Lyall Edeh Herr and my son, Jonathan Edeh Herr for their support of me, especially when I had to squeeze in one more project.

I would like to thank Cindy Ridley and Beverly Schneller for getting me started on the right path.

# PREFACE

Having supervised theses for the past eleven years and having taught research Seminar courses for many years, I learned that everything involved in writing thesis is turning many graduate students away from choosing the thesis option for their Master Programs. This frustration prompted me to write an unpublished workbook for theses, which I used in my class for many years. Many graduate students had asked me to have this workbook published for use as a guide by other graduate students seeking the thesis option.

Those of us who teach advanced courses that result in writing theses and dissertations strive to make the process as simple and easy to follow for educators as possible. Many teachers and other professionals in the field of education are discouraged because of the unnecessary complexity in the process of writing theses and dissertations. Therefore, this workbook is written to focus on the guiding questions in each component of thesis/dissertation and to make the process of writing thesis/dissertation more of a learning experience rather than a frustrating one.

This workbook is intended to compliment other research textbooks of the instructor's choice and to make the process of writing and understanding each components of thesis/dissertation simple for the graduate students.

# CONTENTS

# INTRODUCTION

Before You Begin: Refresh your memory

Many graduate students forget the basic research language before taking their last class which normally leads to writing thesis/dissertation. Therefore, it is important for them to refresh their memories before starting the process of writing.

What is Research? I tell my graduate students that "research brings the world of information together" and it is true. However, many researchers know that the question "what is research?" is not meant to be answered by a single phrase or sentence. When we say research, what exactly does that mean as it relates to writing thesis and dissertation? Thesis/dissertation is not a ten-page paper for which one must use five to ten references any more. The graduate students are about to learn a different meaning of the word "research" now; therefore, it is important to start at the basic steps instead of diving into it with the assumption that they will be okay.

**_<u>What is Research?</u>_** This is a very complicated question that can be answered by addressing different components of research. For the purpose of this workbook, three components will be addressed.

_The first component of research is statistics._ What is statistics? **_<u>Statistics</u>_** is a group of methods used to collect, analyze, present, and interpret data and to make decisions. **Descriptive Statistics** are used to organize and describe data. **_<u>Descriptive Statistics</u>_** consist of methods for organizing, displaying, and describing data by using tables, graphs, and summary measures. **_<u>Inferential Statistics</u>_** consist of methods that use sample results to help make decisions or predictions about a population.

There are three simple steps to doing Statistics correctly: _think, show,_ and _tell_:

<u>Think first.</u> Know where you're heading and why. It will save you a lot of time and frustration. In the space below, write where you think you are heading and why. Keep it simple.

_____

_____

_____

_____

_____

Show is what most people think Statistics is about. While the mechanics of calculating statistics and graphical displays are important, they are not the most important part of Statistics. Since you are at the beginning of this journey, you may not have anything to show yet.

Tell what you've learned. Until you've explained your results so that someone else can understand your conclusions, the job is not done. At this point, you may not have much to tell as it relates to your thesis/dissertation yet.

*The second component of research is population.*

A *population* consists of all elements  individuals, items, or objects—whose characteristics are being studied. For example, your population may be Middle School students: You want to compare the math achievement of students with IEP and students without IEP in the Middle Schools. However, you cannot collect data on all Middle School students in the USA. A portion of the population selected for study is referred to as a **_sample_**. What is your population? Keep in mind that this may change as you move forward with this process.

_____

_____

_____

_____.

*The third component of research is variable.*

It is said that a relationship is a statement about variables. A **_variable_** is a characteristic under study that assumes different values for different elements, units, subjects, or individuals. In other words, a variable is any characteristic that is not always the same; it varies. For example, achievement and gender are variables. <u>Knowledge check:</u> Are brunet students smarter in mathematics than blonde students? What are the variables in this question?

_____

_____

_____

_____.

## Provide an answer to the above research question

What are we saying?

Variables can be classified as qualitative/categorical or quantitative.

  a. Quantitative Variables
      Discrete Variables
      Continuous Variables
  b. Qualitative/Categorical Variables

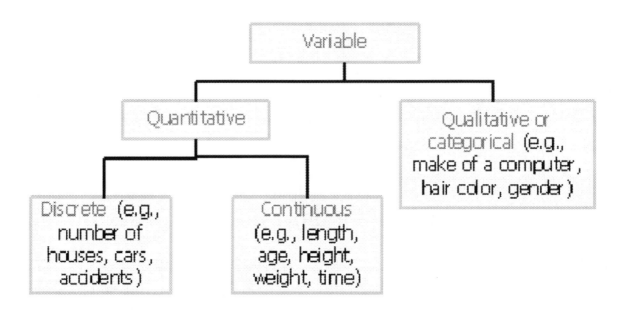

The context of the data we work with is very important. Always think about the "Five W's"—Who, What, When, Where, Why (and How) when reading and examining a set of data.

There are many types of variables, but for the sake of this workbook let me present two of them that you need to know. These two variables are <u>Independent and Dependent variables</u>. The Merriam Webster Dictionary (<u>www.merriam-webster.com</u>) defines Independent variable as *"a mathematical variable that is independent of the other variables in an expression or function and whose value determines one or more of the values of the other variables,"* and it defines Dependent variable as *"a mathematical variable whose value is determined by that of one or more other variables in a function."* If you are like me, you just want it in plain language and how it relates to your study. Let me explain the difference between these two variables using a research question format: *Will students taught by two teachers (in a co-taught classroom) perform better in Math than students taught in a traditional one teacher classroom?* The independent variable is the number of teachers and the dependent variable is the performance (better). In other word, the dependent variable is the outcome. With that in mind, we can define ***Independent variable*** as the one presumed to influence another variable and the other variable affected is **Dependent *variable***. Now that we have this straightened out, write below what you think is your Independent variable(s) and Dependent variable(s).

Independent variable(s):

_____

_____

_____

_____

Dependent variable(s):

_____

_____

_____

_____.

## *Displaying Qualitative Data*

We can "pile" the data by counting the number of data values in each category of interest. We can organize these counts into a frequency table, which records the totals & category names. A relative frequency table is similar, but gives the percentages (instead of counts) for each category.

Frequency tables and relative frequency tables describe the distribution of a categorical variable because they name the possible categories and tell how frequently each occurs. Graphs: Pie Charts & Bar Graphs (software) are used for these types of data.

A contingency table allows us to look at two qualitative variables together.

*Summary:* Qualitative variables can be summarized in frequency or relative frequency tables. Categorical variables can be displayed with bar graphs and/or pie charts. A contingency table summarizes two variables at a time. From a contingency table we can find the marginal distribution for each variable or the conditional distribution for one variable conditioned on the other variable.

## *Displaying Quantitative Data*

Histograms

- First, slice up the entire span of values covered by the quantitative variable into equal-width piles called classes/ bins. "selection = art form"
- The bins and the counts in each bin give the distribution of the quantitative variable.
- One graphical display of the distribution of a quantitative variable is called a histogram, which plots the bin counts as the heights of bars (like a bar graph).
- A relative frequency histogram displays the percentage of cases in each bin instead of the count.

Random Sampling Techniques
- Simple Random Sampling
- Stratified Sampling
- Systematic Sampling
- Cluster Sampling

Data Come from:
- Published Source
- Designed Experiment
- Survey

The purpose of this workbook is to make writing thesis/ dissertation easier and meaningful. Here are some important tips: It is important that you start promptly and remain on target so that you do not fall behind because it is **VERY** difficult to catch up. It is important to receive much feedback from your peers and the professor of the class. Accept this feedback as professional suggestions for your improvement.

## *Let's begin:*

Below is an excellent general format for both quantitative and qualitative studies presented in a guiding-questions format. **Note:** These questions are not official headings for the thesis/dissertation. In some areas when the questions could be topics, quotations marks (" ") will be used. ***Note:*** Your writing should follow either APA or MLA formats. This guide is not meant to replace the professional format used by your program.

**You must choose a topic:** For example, *"Cross-Cultural Investigation of Interest-Based Training and Interpersonal Problem Solving in Students with Mental Retardation"* could be a topic of interest to you. The topic is one of the most important aspects of your thesis/dissertation. Without a workable topic, you may not have a focus. ***Keep in mind that one does not just pick a topic, you combine research with your professional interests and experience to come up with a functional and usable topic.*** No topic is written in stone; therefore, the goal at the beginning is to have a "working" topic. In a space below, jot down possible areas of interest which could be later used as a topic.

_____

_____

_____

_____

_____

_____

_____

_____.

After you have a solid (or working) topic, you will provide a detail rationale for the topic. This means that you professionally tell your readers "why" you think this topic is important and how it will contribute to your field. Remember that the "why" would not be "because I think it is important." You need to have literature/studies supporting your rationale. You will later use part or most of this rationale at the end of Chapter Two when you write the "Rationale for the Present Study."

# CHAPTER I

## Background

For this chapter, **<u>briefly</u>** answer the following questions. Keep in mind that the order in which you answer these questions is not as important as the sequential logic as it relates to your topic. **Note:** These questions are not meant to be answered with yes or no responses.

## I. Do professionals think your topic is important?

**Example from my dissertation:** One of the broadly accepted goals of special education is to help students become competent adults (Perrone & Male, 1981). Competent individuals are "those who manage well the circumstances which they encounter daily, and who possess a judgment which is accurate in meeting occasions as they arise and rarely miss the expedient course of action" (D'Zurilla & Goldfried, 1971). Naisbitt (1982) has suggested that students who are skillful have bright futures because of their ability to meet personal needs while being innovative and useful members of future societies. It continues . . .

Now for your thesis/dissertation jot down brief, but important information in the space provided.

# Do professionals think your topic is important?

_____

_____

_____

_____

_____

_____

_____.

## Sources:

## II. What do the professionals know about your topic and what is the timeline for this knowledge?

**Example from my dissertation:** Since the early 1970s, educators have increased their emphasis on the community placement of individuals with mental retardation (Craighead, Craighead, Kazdin, & Mahoney,1994). With this trend has come the realization that there are a number of skills that facilitate adaptation in community settings. Increasingly, more developmentally advanced skills, such as telephone usage (Risley & Cuvo, 1980), money management (Cuvo, Veitch, Trace, &

Konke, 1978), pedestrian behavior (Page, Iwata, & Neef, 1976), clothing-selection (Nutter & Reid, 1978), cooking (Johnson and Cuvo, 1981), use of fast food restaurants and buses (McDonnell & Ferguson, 1988; Marholin, O'Toole, Touchette, Berger, & Doyle, 1979) have been focused upon in order to facilitate adaptation of individuals with mental retardation into community settings. Initially, investigators working with persons with mental retardation emphasized the training of play skills such as toy contact or toy manipulation (Wehman & Marchant, 1978) and social interactions among children in a play situation (Strain, 1975). Keogh, Faw, Whitman, and Reid (1984) employed a treatment package consisting of modeling, verbal and physical prompts, and corrective feedback to train adolescent boys with severe mental retardation to play with commercial games.

## What do the professionals know about your topic and what is the timeline for this knowledge?

_____

_____

_____

_____

_____

_____

_____ .

**Sources:**

# III. What are the professionals doing about your topic?

**Example from my dissertation:** With the emphasis on sheltered and supported employment, a number of studies have concentrated on developing work and work-related skills in individuals with mental retardation (Gold, 1972, 1976). Training programs have focused on teaching a variety of simple and more complex job skills, such as sorting different sized bolts and assembling bicycle brakes (Gold, 1972).

In addition to teaching specific job skills, research has focused on maintaining and increasing work output. A variety of procedures have been evaluated in the past studies, including differentially reinforcing higher rates of work (Bellamy, Inman, & Yates, 1978); changing the latency of reinforcement by decreasing pay periods from one month to one week (Martin & Morris, 1980); increasing the amount of money per task (Bates, Renzagalia, & Clees,1980); and manipulating antecedent stimuli, such as providing specific job information and reducing environmental distractions through use of partitions (Martin, Palltta-Cornick, Johnstone, & Goyos, 1980).

## What are the professionals doing about your topic?

_____

_____

_____

_____

_____

_____

_____.

**Sources:**

# IV. Are professionals having problems in what they are doing?

**Example from my dissertation:** While problem solving is accepted as one of the basic skills children need, generally, it is not taught as such in most schools (Dolman & Williamson, 1983). The general method used to teach problem solving according to Treffinger, Speedie and Burner (1974) has been to follow a particular technique or to set steps, such as translating word problems into equations (Kaufman, 1979). The transferability of specific instruction to other problem sets is questionable (Treffinger et al. 1974). An example of this comes from the study by Treffinger et al. (1974) that used a test of problem solving as a criterion measure and found no growth in ability to solve real-life school problems.

## Are professionals having problems in what they are doing?

_____

_____

_____

_____

_____

_____

_____.

**Sources:**

# V. Do professionals neglect important aspects of your topic?

**Example from my dissertation:** A complication related to problem solving behavior is that various cultures emphasize different modes of problem solving. There is overwhelming evidence that culture plays an important role in children's cognition and that different cultures promote different learning styles and problem solving strategies based on their cultural values and backgrounds. However, no study was found to suggest whether culture plays any role in the problem solving of individuals with mental retardation or whether any particular cognitive strategy is more effective than others in training individuals with mental retardation from different cultural backgrounds to problem solve in social interpersonal situations.

# Do professionals neglect important aspects of your topic?

_____

_____

_____

_____

_____

_____

_____.


**Sources:**


**VI. If needed, provide descriptions/ and or definitions of terminologies you will use in this study.**


**Example from my dissertation:**


<u>Definition of Problem Solving and Decision Making</u>


Problem solving is broadly defined by Anderson (1985) as the active process of trying to change the existing state of a situation into a desired state. Any problem situation contains three important characteristics: givens, a goal, and obstacles and define givens, a goal, and obstacles.

Decision making, on the other hand, has been defined as the process of making choices among competing courses of action (Band & Weisz, 1988). Decision making involves more than just an expression of preferences, it is also an understanding of an issue, identification and evaluation of options, communication of a decision, and a commitment to action (Jenkinson & Nelms, 1994).

**Provide <u>detailed</u> definitions to terminologies you will use in this study/paper.**

_____

_____

_____

_____

_____

_____

_____.

**Sources:**

# VII. Provide a brief statement why the above definitions are important.

**Example from my dissertation:** In the definitions of problem solving and decision making above, a person must decide on a course of action to meet a need or solve a conflict in an encountered situation. However, the obstacles in the problem solving definition are not present in the decision making definition.

## Provide a brief statement why the above definitions are important.

_____

_____

_____

_____

_____

_____

_____.

**Sources:**

# VIII. If the above definitions have multiple components, state, define, and provide examples of them here.

**Example from my dissertation:**

<u>Types of Problem Solving</u>

There are many types of problem solving. For the sake of this study, three types (abstract, concrete, and social interpersonal) will be discussed with the emphasis on social interpersonal problem solving. Problem solving is important to school achievement and important in everyday life. There are many instances where children and adults have to solve problems daily, using either abstract, concrete, or social interpersonal problem solving skills.

Abstract problem solving is defined as . . .

Concrete problem solving, on the other hand, is defined synonymously with information processing . . .

Social interpersonal problem solving is the ability to generate . . .

## If the above definitions have multiple components, state, define, and provide examples of them here.

_____

_____

_____

_____

_____

_____

_____.


**Sources:**


## IX. Remember question V. above (Do professionals neglect important aspects of your topic)? Define and strongly connect it to your topic.


**Example from my dissertation:**


Culture, Cognition, and Problem Solving


Cole (1988) found, based on his experimental studies of Kpelle people, that cultural differences in cognition reside more in the situations to which particular cognitive processes are applied than in the existence of a process in one cultural group and its absence in another.

Culture, according to Shade and Edwards (1987), is defined as the collective consciousness of a community with its own unique customs, rituals, communication style, coping patterns, and social organization. This definition is important because it illustrates the pervasive influence of culture on people's values, attitudes, beliefs, behaviors, and approach to problem solving.

**<u>Remember question V. above (Do professionals neglect important aspects of your topic)? Define and strongly connect it to your topic.</u>**

_____

_____

_____

_____

_____

_____.

**Sources:**

## X. Now that you've proven that your topic is important, provide "The Statement of the Problem"

**Example from my dissertation:**

There is considerable research suggesting that the poor community adjustment of many adults with mental retardation is due as much to deficits in social competence as to limited intellectual abilities (Zigler & Harter, 1969) . . . . According to D'Zurilla and Goldfried (1971), the goal in developing problem-solving skills is to train an individual in resolving new problems as they arise, rather than solving a single problem. Also, participants in Castles and Glass' study are adults with mental retardation, not children. Additionally, there was no indication that culture was a component in their study . . . .

There is overwhelming evidence that culture plays an important role in children's cognition and that different cultures promote different learning styles and problem solving strategies based on their cultural values and backgrounds. However, no study was found to suggest whether culture plays any role in the problem solving of individuals with mental retardation or whether any particular cognitive strategy is more effective than others in training individuals with mental retardation from different cultural backgrounds to problem solve in social interpersonal situations . . . .

## Now that you've proven that your topic is important, provide "The Statement of the Problem"

_____

_____

_____

_____

_____

_____

_____.

### Sources:

**Note:** Generally, Chapter one should not be in depth, but this depends on your study. Some theses/dissertations may have ten (10) pages for chapter one while others may have more or less, depending on the topic.

# CHAPTER II

## REVIEW OF THE LITERATURE

For this chapter, answer the following questions in **detail**. Keep in mind that the order in which you answer these questions is not as important as the sequential logic as it relates to your paper (topic). **Note:** Some of the information here may overlap with the information in chapter one.

**I. Provide an overview of chapter two. Keep in mind that you do not label it as such. Note:** This part is usually written last.

**Example from my dissertation:** This literature review is organized into six parts: The first part describes the theories and research on problem solving with the focus on general problem solving. The second part describes theories and research on social problem solving. The emphasis here is on two areas: The limitations of the existing strategies used to teach social interpersonal problem solving to students with mental retardation from different cultural backgrounds and the effectiveness of general cognitive strategies used to train social interpersonal problem solving skills to individuals with mental retardation. The third part describes theories and research on culture and problem solving with the focus on African-Americans and Euro-Americans. The fourth part describes Nigerian culture. The fifth part describes

Euro-American culture. The sixth part is the summary of the research followed by the rationale for the present study and the research questions.

**Provide an overview of chapter two. Keep in mind that you do not label it as such. Note: This part is usually written last.**

_____

_____

_____

_____

_____

_____

_____.

**II. What is the literature regarding the theories surrounding your topic? Note:** This section is usually detailed.

**Example from my dissertation:**

# General Problem Solving

Problem solving is important in all cultures. Almost everything that an individual does involves solving problems, or behavior that is directed toward achieving a goal (Anderson, 1985) . . . .

Research in problem solving has come from several different fields, including experimental psychology, education, and industry . . . . In an attempt to explain why some people have difficulties in making the appropriate decisions when they encounter problem situations, three problem solving models are examined: behavioral models, cognitive models, and cognitive-behavioral models. Each of these models is briefly described below.

## Behavioral Models

Behavioral models of problem solving examine the motivational forces, the processes that contribute to and shape behaviors, the degree to which external events influence an individual's life, and the degree to which the influence of such events can be modified . . . .

## Cognitive Models

The first cognitive revolution is said to have taken place in the decade between 1955 and 1965. That was the "information processing revolution", and it remains the best known phase of cognitive science (Craighead et al., 1994) . . . .

## Cognitive-Behavioral Models

The behavioral approach tries to avoid unverifiable, unobservable inner states. However, according to Craighead et al. (1994), it would be inaccurate to state that internal states are avoided altogether . . . . D'Zurilla and Goldfried (1971) stated, "It should now be clear that the goals of problem solving and behavior modification are one and the same, namely, to stimulate behavior which is likely to produce positive consequences, that is, positive reinforcement, and avoid negative consequences, that is, negative reinforcement" (p. 109) . . . .

# Social Problem Solving

## Models and Theories

Social skills training is based on the theory that poor competence is often the result of deficits in specific verbal and/or nonverbal skills necessary for effective social interaction (Hersen & Eisler, 1976). **Same pattern as above. After that, you connect those theories to your population of interest.**

## Mental Retardation

The model of social competence by Greenspan and Granfield (1992) addresses one of the components in the definition of mental retardation . . . . The model of social competence contains two major subdivisions: Social competence and instrumental competence. These subdivisions each have intellectual and nonintellectual components (See Figure 1). **Include important figures from your literature review when appropriate. Note:** Whether you adapt the figures and use the original version, remember to give credit to the author(s).

# What is the literature regarding the theories surrounding your topic? Note: This section is usually detailed.

In the space below, list possible theories that you are considering.

_____

_____

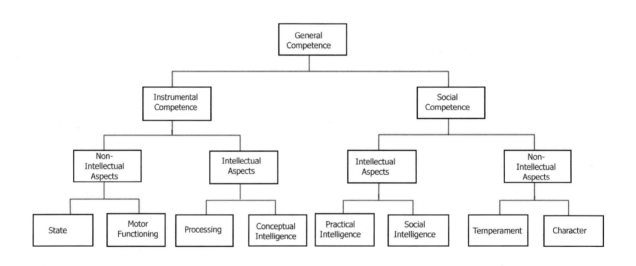

**Figure 1:** Comprehensive model of general competence (Greenspan & Granfield, 1992)

_____

_____

_____

_____

_____

_____

_____

_____.

## III. What is the literature regarding the studies surrounding your topic? Note: This section is usually detailed.

**Example from my dissertation:** When you finish with the theories, you continue in the same manner, but with the actual studies done regarding your topic. You might want to focus on the actual studies/trainings in this section. **Note:** *Example in this section is long to give you a clearer view on how to use the existing studies as foundation for your study.*

Social Skills Training

Social skills training programs have been successfully used to help people with mental retardation become more assertive

(Bregman, 1984; Stacy, Doleys, & Malcolm, 1979), improve their social skills and improve general interpersonal skills (Bates, 1980; Foxx, McMorrow, & Schloss, 1983; Senatore, Matson, & Kazdin, 1982). Interpersonal problem-solving training, based on the work of D'Zurilla and Goldfried (1971) and Spivack, Platt, and Shure (1976), teaches the process of problem solving rather than the content of solutions to specific problems . . . .

Many methods and strategies have been used in teaching individuals with mental retardation to problem solve. An example of this is the video clip approach, used by Browning and Nave (1993), to successfully promote these skills in students with mild mental retardation. They used 33 video scenarios and 65 slides in five lessons to field test a curriculum for teaching social problem solving skills to 104 secondary students with mild mental retardation . . . .

Castles and Glass (1986) examined social and interpersonal problem solving skills for adults with mild and moderate mental retardation. They included 33 adults with mild and moderate mental retardation who were clients in a vocational training facility in a large metropolitan area. They gave three different types of skills: social skills training, interpersonal problem solving training, and a combination of the two . . . . Although the results of the Castles and Glass (1986) study were encouraging, the treatment gains did not generalize into the untrained role-play situations. Strategies for generalization, which teach a general process for dealing with interpersonal problems, should be more likely to generalize to real-life behavior than will social-skills training, which teaches the content of effective responses to specific problem situations.

**Note:** As you can see from the way this section is written, in addition to giving the authors credit for their work and represent their studies, its results accurately, this is also when you "poke holes" in the existing studies to make "pave way" for your study.

## Cultural Differences in Problem Solving

### Culture and Cognitive Style

The components of a culture are built upon a basic philosophical world view . . . . Cole (1988) suggested that the human mind functions the same everywhere, but the way it "behaves" in response to any particular stimulus is culturally determined . . . .

## Field Dependence and Independence

The term "field-dependence" derives from the original research on the rod-and-frame experiment in which a rod was suspended inside a square frame. Under control conditions, the rod would point to opposite vertices of the frame. Under experimental conditions, the frame would be tilted slightly so that the rod no longer pointed to the frame's vertices. Field dependent participants would indicate counter factually that the rod was tilted. Field independent participants would indicate that the rod was still pointing perpendicularly (Goldstein & Blackman, 1978). See Figure 2 for rod-and-frame control and experimental conditions.

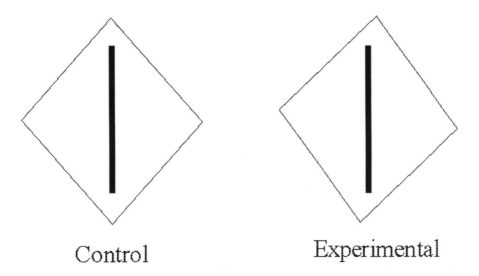

Control                    Experimental

**Figure 2:**        Control and experimental conditions of the
                    rod-and-frame experiment

Continue until you finish all relevant studies needed to support
your study.

**What is the literature regarding the studies surrounding
your topic?** Note: This section is usually detailed.

In the space below, write the headings/subheadings in outline
form the studies surrounding your topic.

_____

_____

_____

_____

_____

_____

_____

_____

_____

_____

_____

_____

_____

_____

_____

_____

_____ .

# IV. When you finish with the literature review, provide the summary and rationale for your study.

## Example from my dissertation:

## Summary

This review began with the description of three theoretical models of problem solving: behavioral models, cognitive models, and cognitive-behavioral models. A social problem solving model was also examined in light of the proposed re-definition of mental retardation as "subaverage intellectual abilities that are reflected in significant deficits in the ability to succeed in roles and activities essential in an individual's primary culture" (Greenspan, Granfield, & Becker, 1991). Finally, the relationship between culture, cognition and problem solving were introduced with emphasis on African-American, Nigerian, and Euro-American cultures.

There is considerable research suggesting that the poor community adjustment of many adults with mental retardation is due as much to deficits in social competence as to limited intellectual abilities . . . .

In the literature reviewed for this study, many researchers agreed that external factors, such as culture, play an important role in children's cognition and problem solving abilities. Geary (1995) presented two general classes of cognitive ability which he labeled as biologically primary cognitive abilities and biologically secondary cognitive abilities. The development of biologically secondary cognitive abilities reflected the co-optation of primary abilities for purposes other than the original evolution-based function and seemed to develop only in specific cultural contexts. These abilities do not appear to have the same biological advantages as biologically primary cognitive abilities. The acquisition of biologically secondary cognitive abilities, is generally slow, effortful, and occurs only with sustained formal and informal instruction (Gelman, 1993).

The interest for the present study emerged out of the differences and similarities that exist in African-American, Nigerian, and Euro-American students. Literature were presented that suggested that the cognitive styles of African-American students were different than those of Euro-American students, and that schools were organized to utilize the cognitive modes of Euro-American students, placing African-American students at a relative disadvantage to Euro-American students . . . .

# Example from my dissertation:

# Rationale for the Present Study

As seen from the literature, biologically secondary cognitive abilities or external factors, which contribute to problem solving abilities, occur only with sustained formal and informal instruction. It is therefore appropriate to suggest that individuals with mental retardation who are from different cultural backgrounds, could be trained using a general cognitive strategy to solve problems to their full potential.

There is overwhelming evidence, that culture plays an important role in children's cognition and that different cultures promote different learning styles and problem solving strategies based on their cultural values and backgrounds. *However, there was no study found to suggest whether culture plays any role in the problem solving of individuals with mental retardation or whether any particular cognitive strategy is more effective in training these individuals from different cultural backgrounds to problem solve in social interpersonal situations.* Also, most of the general cognitive strategy training in social interpersonal situations has been done with adults with mental retardation. Training children with mental retardation to use general cognitive strategies to problem solve might be more effective and beneficial as the skills learned may carry over into their adult lives.

The present study has two primary purposes. The first purpose is to investigate whether children with mild mental retardation solve problems in a way that is consistent with their cultural values and backgrounds. The second purpose is to investigate the effectiveness of general cognitive problem solving strategy training based on the work of D'Zurilla and Goldfried (1971) and Spivack, Platt, and Shure (1977)using an interest-based method vs. traditional method. This approach is designed to teach the process of problem solving rather than the content of solutions to specific problems. The intent of this training is to empower African-American students with mild mental retardation to employ an effective process of problem solving, and to investigate the sex differences in problem solving style African-American students.

When you finish with the summary and rationale for the present study, then you finalize your research questions. Some professionals had asked me why I use research questions instead of developing a hypothesis. Research questions allow graduate students to start and remain focused because the research questions are direct and to the point. In addition, research questions provide graduate students the flexibility of developing their theoretical framework and reporting the results of their studies without the feeling of being "let down" if the hypothesis proves null. Any outcome of a study is useful.

## V. Chapter two of your thesis/dissertation should end with research questions.

**Example from my dissertation:**

## Research Questions

The present two-phased study was designed to answer the following questions:

## Phase I:

1a.    Will problem solving performance differ for children from the three cultures (Nigerian, African-American, and Euro-American)?

1b.    Will problem solving style differ for children from the three cultures (Nigerian, African-American, and Euro-American)?

2a.  Will problem solving performance differ for males vs. females?

2b.  Will problem solving style differ for males vs. females?

3a.  Will there be any interactions between culture and sex for problem solving performance?

3b.  Will there be any interactions between culture and sex for problem solving style?

## Phase II:

4.  Will the problem solving performance of African-American children differ after participating in one of the three training conditions (interest-based method vs. traditional method vs. control group)?

5.  Will problem solving performance differ for males vs. females?

6.  Will there be any interactions among the effects of sex and training conditions?

7.  Will there be any correlations between performance on the dependent variables and years in school and training conditions?

# Write draft research questions for your thesis/dissertation here.

_____

_____

_____

_____

_____

_____

_____

_____.

# CHAPTER III

## METHOD

The initial write-up of chapter three is usually brief and written in future tense. It is a proposed methodology for your study. After your study, you then re-write (using appropriate tenses, including present, past, etc.) or expand your proposed methodology to reflect the actual method used in your study. Below are the important components of chapter three.

## I. Participants: who you will be using for your study. Age, sex, disability (ies), demographic Characteristics, etc.

**Example from my dissertation:**

Participants

Prior to the study, the researchers sent and received all consent forms from the parent(s) or guidance and the school authorities. The 72 participants were balanced across three cultures: Twenty-four Nigerians (living in Nigeria), 24 African-Americans, and 24 non-Hispanic Euro-Americans. Equal numbers of male and female participants who were classified as having mild mental retardation (IQ 55-70) were selected for each cultural sample. All the participants had been attending special education schools/classes for at least five years and at most 10 years. The ages of the participants ranged from nine to 15. The participants were matched in age and time in school across the cultures. All participants were required to meet the following criteria in order to establish the comparability of the students across the three cultures:

**Table 1** (You may want to use a Table to display the number as well)

## Participants' Demographic Characteristics by Cultural Group and Overall

| Ethnicity | Males (n=36) | Females (n=36) | Public Sch. | Private Sch. | Overall (n=72) |
|---|---|---|---|---|---|
| African-American (n=24) | 16.67% | 16.67% | (18) 25% | (6) 8.34% | 33.34% |
| Euro-American (n=24) | 16.67% | 16.67% | (20) 27.78% | (4) 5.56% | 33.34% |
| Nigerian (n=24) | 16.67% | 16.67% | (5) 6.95% | (19) 26.39% | 33.34% |
| Total (n=72) | 50% | 50% | (43) 59.73% | (29) 40.29% | 100% |

# Participants for your study: who you will be using for your study. Age, sex, disability (ies), demographic Characteristics, etc.

_____

_____

_____

_____

_____

_____

_____

_____.

## II. Instrumentation: what instrument (s) will you be using in your study/data collection?

This section is where you list any and all instruments you will be using for your study.

**Example from my dissertation:**

Archival Materials

The materials for this study included the IQ scores (or psychologists' report when IQ scores were not available), students' portfolios and other progress reports in the students' files. This insured that all the participants met the criteria for the study. These materials were reviewed in advance before the participants were selected. Prior to the study, the researcher sent and received all consent forms from the parent(s) or guidance and school authorities.

Edeh Scale of Interpersonal Problem Situations

Social interpersonal problem solving tasks were used in this study. Ten social interpersonal problem solving vignettes were used for the assessment in Phase I. All Phase II participants were pretested and posttested on the 10 vignettes. There were both male and female targets used to depict children of the same sex as the participant.

The vignettes were very short, involving three to four sentences. An example is: "You are playing a basketball game. Your friend came in the middle of the game. Your friend wants to join in the game." The participant was then asked to state how many ways he or she could solve the problem. As the participant listed the different possible solutions, the examiner wrote them on a list on the interview schedule. Then the examiner stated, "Let me give you four other ways to solve the same problem." Then the examiner stated the four alternatives . . . .

Scoring (you may create your own scoring or adapt it from the published one. If adapting, remember to give credit to the author).

Scoring was adapted from the coding system designed by Band and Weisz (1988) to score children's coping behavior. For the purpose of this study, four scoring categories were used. The chosen categories deal with how a child would respond if he or she were faced with any problem situation and there was a need to solve the problem at hand.

Scoring was as follows: First, the number of spontaneous alternatives in response to the first question of how many ways the participant could solve the problem was counted over the 10 vignettes. Second, the responses to the multiple choice items were scored by counting the number of CI responses, II problem solving responses, OD problem solving responses, and AV responses. The four problem solving modes, then, summed to 10. Third, the spontaneous responses to the first question was coded using cooperative/negotiation independent (CI) strategy, an individualistic independent (II) strategy, an other-dependent (OD) strategy, an avoidance (AV) strategy, compliance, and other . . . .

## Reliability Coefficients

The reliability coefficient of the instrument using the procedure from the Statistical Package for the Social Sciences (SPSS) software was used to show an index of how reliable the instrument is. The alpha is based on the internal consistency of the test. That is, it is based on the average covariance among items on the instrument. The overall reliability coefficients were: Avoidance responses=

83.0%; Other-dependent responses=78.4%, Independent individualist responses=76.6%, and Independent cooperative/negotiation responses=80.3%.

## Interscorer Reliability

Fifty percent of the pretest of social interpersonal problem solving vignettes were scored independently by two scorers: the researcher and a doctoral candidate from NYU. Differences in scores were discussed and scoring criteria was clarified. Using the revised scoring system, all social interpersonal problem solving vignettes both phase I and phase II were then scored independently by the two scorers. Interscorer percentage of agreement, calculated separately for the phase I and phase II of scores, was obtained by dividing the number of agreements by the total of agreements and disagreements multiplied by 100. The interscorer agreement for phase I were: African-American=93.9%, Euro-American=96.4%, and Nigerian=89.8% and phase II was 92.70%. Scores given by the NYU doctoral candidate were used in the data analyses.

**Instrumentation: what instrument (s) will you be using in your study/data collection?** List (just the names of) any and all instruments you will be using for your study here.

_____

_____

_____

_____

_____

_____

_____

_____

_____.

# III. Procedure: what are the processes you will follow for your study? Note: Don't assume that some processes are common knowledge.

**Example from my dissertation:**

<u>Training of the Examiners</u>

The researcher and those helping her are referred to as the "examiners." Prior to participation in the study, all the examiners participated in four hours of training given by the researcher to familiarize them with the social interpersonal problem solving materials and also to understand what was expected of them. Examiners were instructed in the methods by which the problem solving interview was to be conducted. Examiners participated in mock interviews as part of their training.

<u>Data Collection</u>

After a brief greeting, the examiner told each participant that the purpose of the interview was to see how many different ways he or she could think of solving a problem. All participants were interviewed individually in an isolated room within their schools by the researcher or by one of the trained examiners. The examiner slowly read a social interpersonal problem situation from the vignette, then asked the participant, "How many ways do you think this problem can be solved?" The examiner wrote each participant's responses down in the space provided for each problem situation. Although there were no probes during the testing, the examiner asked, "Are you finished?" before she or he proceeded to the next step of the interview. After that, the examiner provided each participant with four alternative ways to solve the same problem and asked the participant to choose one of the given alternatives. When a session was finished, the examiner thanked the participant and said, "This session is finished". This procedure was followed during Phase I and Phase II assessments.

## Experimental Treatment: Phase II

The two African-American treatment groups each received a total of 10 training sessions; each session was conducted in a small group of 4 or 5 students. The training sessions on solving social interpersonal problem situations were taught by the researcher. See Appendix C for details of the training sessions. **(Always refer to the appendixes when appropriate.)** . . . .

The examiner used the general stages of problem solving by D'Zurilla and Goldfried (1971) which include teaching problem identification, evaluating the problem, generating alternative solutions to the problem, deciding among the alternatives, and evaluating the outcome of the solution.

There were 10 training sessions with the experimental groups. The interest-based materials were used in the training of the interest-based treatment group. For example, one small group's interest may be sports (e.g., soccer). The givens (original state), was a display of a soccer field with a person and a ball in the middle of the field. The goal was the ball going in to the net at the end zone of the soccer field. This was displayed by an arrow showing the ball in the net. The obstacles were the opponents who were pictured blocking and preventing the ball from going into the net.

## The Control Group

The control group did not participate in the training at all. They participate only in the pretest and the posttest when participants in the two treatment groups were assessed.

## For your study:

## Procedure: what are the processes you will follow for your study? Note: Don't assume that some processes are common knowledge.

_____

_____

_____

_____

_____

_____

_____

_____.

# IV. Analysis of the Data: now you tell your reader(s) your proposed data analysis. This may change slightly with the actual data analysis, but stay within your proposal.

## Example from my dissertation:

The design for this study consisted of two phases. Phase one investigated cultural differences in problem solving performance and problem solving styles on social interpersonal problem-solving vignettes among African-American, Euro-American, and Nigerian students in social interpersonal problem situations. Phase two examined the effects of two training methods (interest-based and traditional) in improving participants' independent problem solving skills in response to social interpersonal problem situations.

<u>Phase I</u>

The Seventy-two (72) participants for the phase one study were from 3 cultural groups (African-American, Euro American, and Nigerian) with equal numbers of females and males within cultures. See Table 2 for demographic characteristics for cultural groups. All the participants met the screening criteria which included an IQ within the range from 55-70 and at least 75% correct responses on the comprehension test (see appendix A for comprehension test).

Preliminary Analyses included means and standard deviations (SDs)of participants' age, years in school, IQ scores, and comprehension scores by cultural groups. Analysis of variance was used to analyze the data for phase one. Cultural groups (African-American, Euro-American, and Nigerian) and sex were between subjects factors. A 3 (cultures) x 2 (sex) analysis of variance on spontaneous and multiple choice independent (correct) responses on problem solving performance was performed. Separate 3 (cultures) x 2 (sex) multivariate analyses of variance (MANOVA) on two transformed style scores for spontaneous and multiple choice problem solving responses were performed to compare the groups on their problem solving styles. The formulas for the two transformed style scores were: 1) independent/non-independent problem solving styles = individualistic independent problem solving responses + cooperative independent problem solving responses—2 x (nonindependent problem solving responses). According to this formula all independent responses were added and all non-independent responses were multiplied by two, then subtracted from the independent responses. 2) individualistic/

cooperative problem solving style = individualistic independent problem solving styles—cooperative independent problem solving styles. This formula looks only at the independent responses. The independent problem solving score was the sum of cooperative problem solving and individualistic problem solving scores. Therefore, when the cooperative independent problem solving score was subtracted from the individualistic independent problem solving score, it yielded the individualistic/cooperative problem solving style.

## Phase II

A 3 x 2 Analysis of covariance (ANCOVA) was used to analyze the data for phase two. Treatment groups (interest-based training, traditional training, and control group) and sex (male vs. female) were the between-subjects factors. Analysis of covariance was used to compare the effects of training on participants' spontaneous and multiple choice independent problem solving performance (correct responses) as measured on the social interpersonal problem solving vignettes. The analysis of covariance included the posttest scores of spontaneous (self-generated) and multiple choice (selected) independent problem solving performance as the dependent variables and the pretest scores of spontaneous and multiple choice independent problem solving performance as covariates.

**For your study:**

**Analysis of the Data: now you tell your reader(s) your proposed data analysis. This may change slightly with the actual data analysis, but stay within your proposal.**

_____

_____

_____

_____

_____

_____

_____

_____

_____ .

# CHAPTER IV

## RESULTS

In this chapter, present your results. As you can see from the example below, you want to remind the readers of some of the information from chapter three. **Note:** Information in chapter four is clearly and objectively stated from the results. This is not where you discuss what you think the results mean; that is chapter five.

**Example from my dissertation:**

The design for this study consisted of two phases. Phase one investigated cultural differences in problem solving performance and problem solving styles on social interpersonal problem-solving vignettes among African-American, Euro-American, and Nigerian students in social interpersonal problem situations. Phase two examined the effects of two training methods (interest-based and traditional) in improving participants' independent problem solving skills in response to social interpersonal problem situations. Phase two training was done with African-American participants only. Problem solving performance was assessed in terms of spontaneous (self-generated) and multiple choice (selected) independent responses for both phases one and two.

## Alternatives Generated by the Participants

All the participants responded to social interpersonal problem solving vignettes. Individuals with mental retardation are said to generate limited number of alternatives compared to those without mental retardation. This was found to be so with the present study involving three cultural groups. Participants in both phase one and phase two of this study did not generate many alternatives. Therefore, the first response (alternative) given by each participant who generated more than one alternative was used as the response for the analysis of this study. Cross-tabulation was done to count the numbers of alternatives generated by the participants. Most students who generated more than one alternative restated the first alternative. For example, seven of the 24 African-Americans in phase one generated two alternatives. However, six of those seven restated the first alternative. Four Euro-Americans generated two alternatives and all of them restated the first alternative. Eight Nigerians generated two alternatives and two generated three alternatives. Those who generated more than one alternative did not do so across the 10 vignettes. Multiple alternatives ranged from one to 4 vignettes with the average of two vignettes per student. The following is one example of restating alternative: Vignette #1 "You are riding your bicycle in the park (playground). Your friend wants to ride your bike. But you still want to ride your bike. State how many ways you can solve this problem." Participant responded, alternative #1, "No, not now, wait." #2, "Later when I finish." Though the participant above provided 2 alternatives, the second alternative appeared to restate or clarify the first alternative. Either of the above alternatives fall into the independent problem solving style; therefore, the first one was used in the data entry.

Analysis of variance was used to analyze the data for phase one. Cultural groups (African-American, Euro-American, and Nigerian) and sex were between subjects factors. A 3 (cultures) x 2 (sex) analysis of variance on spontaneous and multiple choice independent (correct) responses on problem solving performance was performed. Separate 3 (cultures) x 2 (sex) multivariate analyses of variance (MANOVA) on two transformed scores for spontaneous and multiple choice problem solving responses were performed to compare the groups on their problem solving styles. The formulas for the two transformed style scores were: 1) independent/non-independent problem solving styles = individualistic independent problem solving responses + cooperative independent problem solving responses—2 x (nonindependent problem solving responses).

According to this formula all independent responses were added and all non-independent responses were multiplied by two, then subtracted from the independent responses. 2) individualistic/cooperative problem solving style = individualistic independent problem solving styles—cooperative independent problem solving styles. This formula looks only at the independent responses. The independent problem solving score was the sum of cooperative problem solving and individualistic problem solving scores. Therefore, when the cooperative independent problem solving score was subtracted from the individualistic independent problem solving score, it yielded the individualistic/cooperative problem solving style.

A 3 x 2 Analysis of covariance (ANCOVA) was used to analyze the data for phase two. Treatment groups (interest-based training, traditional training, and control group) and sex (male vs. female) were the between-subjects factors. Analysis of covariance was used to compare the effects of training on participants' spontaneous and multiple choice independent problem solving performance (correct responses) as measured on the social interpersonal problem solving vignettes. The analysis of covariance included the posttest scores of spontaneous (self-generated) and multiple choice (selected) independent problem solving performance as the dependent variables and the pretest scores of spontaneous and multiple choice independent problem solving performance as covariates.

Additional analyses examined the frequencies and percents of non-independent (error) problem solving performance categories (other-dependent, avoidance, compliance, and other) for males and females across the 3 cultural groups for phase 1 and for males and females across the 3 treatment groups for phase 2.

## Phase I

Preliminary Analyses

Means and standard deviations (SDs) of participants' age, years in school, IQ, and comprehension scores by cultural groups are presented in Table 4. One-way ANOVAs for years in school, age, and comprehension scores, presented in Tables 5—7, failed to reveal any significant mean differences among the cultural groups. The IQ score for the cultural groups are as follows: African-American ranged from 55-70 and mean of 64.50; Euro-American ranged from 55-70 and mean of 64.50; and Nigerian ranged from 57-65 and mean of 60.35. Though the Nigerian students had lower IQ scores and the ANOVA, presented in Table 8, is significant, there were seven IQ scores not reported among the Nigerians. Therefore, one can not be certain that the Nigerian students were lower than both African-American and Euro-American students. More so, the three groups did not differ in their comprehension; so it is appropriate to assume that the three groups were comparable.

## Main Analysis

Differences on spontaneous and multiple choice independent problem solving performance among cultural groups were examined using 3 (cultural groups) x 2 (sex) ANOVAs. Means and standard deviations of participants' spontaneous and multiple choice independent (correct) problem solving performance and problem solving styles on social interpersonal problem solving vignettes are presented in Table 9, 12, and 15.

## Research Question #1a

Will problem solving performance differ for the three cultures (African-American, Euro-American, and Nigerian)?

The summary of the 3 (cultural groups) x 2 (sex) analysis of variance for participants' spontaneous and multiple choice problem solving performance on social interpersonal problem solving vignettes are presented in Tables 10 and 11. There was a significant main effect indicating cultural group differences for participants' spontaneous problem solving performance $F(2,66)=$ 8.774, p<.000) only. There were no significant differences in multiple choice problem solving performance.

# Phase 2

## Preliminary Data Analysis

The Seventy-two (72) participants for the phase two study were all African-Americans. See Table 3 for demographic characteristics for the treatment groups. All the participants met the screening criteria which included an IQ within the range from 55-70 and obtained at least, 75% correct on the comprehension test.

Means and standard deviations (SDs) of participants' age, years in school, comprehension and IQ scores by treatment groups are presented in Table 20. One-way ANOVAs for these scores, presented in Tables 21—24, failed to reveal any significant mean differences among the treatment groups. All the participants responded to the social interpersonal problem solving vignettes (pretest and posttest) to determine the effects of training on their problem solving performance by comparing the three training conditions (interest-based method, traditional method, and control group).

Means and standard deviations (SDs)of participants' pretest-posttest and adjusted posttest scores by treatment groups and sex are presented in Table 25. A 3 x 2 ANOVA for pretest scores, presented in Table 26, failed to reveal any significant differences among the treatment groups and sex within the treatment.

Pearson correlational analyses included pretest and posttest scores for all dependent measures to test the analysis of covariance design (ANCOVA) assumptions of linearity and homogeneity of within-group regression. The spontaneous independent pretest and posttest scores were correlated at $r = .572$ ($p < .01$) for interest-based group, $r = .390$ for traditional group, $r = .364$ for control group, and overall $r = .264$ ($p < .05$) respectfully. The multiple choice independent pretest and posttest scores were correlated at $r = .241$ for interest-based group, $r = .582$ ($p < .01$) for traditional group, $r = .145$ for control group, and overall $r = .168$ respectfully. There were positive pre-post test correlations within each treatment group which warranting the use of ANCOVA for the main posttest analyses. The results are presented in Table 27.

## Summary of the Results

Significant differences were found in problem solving performances among the three cultures. Overall, Nigerians produced more spontaneous independent responses than Euro-Americans and African-Americans and Euro-Americans produced more spontaneous independent responses than African-Americans. However, Euro-Americans selected more multiple choice independent responses followed by African-Americans and Nigerians selected fewer independent problem solving responses. The findings indicated that Nigerian students were significantly less individualistic in their social problem solving styles than either African-American or Euro-American students.

Significant gender differences were found on both spontaneously generated social problem solutions and multiple choice solutions. In both cases, males chose more independent problem solving strategies than females. Also, males had more independent problem solving styles in both spontaneous and multiple choice responses, than did female students. There were no gender differences on individualistic styles.

There was a gender by cultural group interaction that indicated that among Nigerians, females made significantly fewer independent choices on the multiple choice items than did Nigerian males. A similar trend existed in the spontaneous choices. The findings indicated that Nigerian and Euro-American males had significantly stronger independent problem solving styles than females; however, there were no differences between African-American males and females.

The data indicated that interest-based method generated significantly higher posttest independent responses than both the traditional method and the control group and the traditional method generated more independent responses than the control group on both spontaneous and multiple choice responses on social problem solving responses. The number of spontaneous independent responses was positively correlated with the number of years in school. There was no significant relationship between years in school and multiple choice responses.

# CHAPTER V

## DISCUSSION

**Note:** This chapter is where you elaborate on the results. In your professional opinion, what are the results telling you? Connect this with literature that you've used in chapter two if needed. Remember that your professional opinion must be rooted in the literature.

**Example from my dissertation:**

The present study supports several theoretical frameworks presented in Chapter II. TenHouten (1971) has suggested that within a social order, cognitive styles can vary by ethnicity and social class, and that social privilege may be associated with certain cognitive skills. The distinctions among these abilities have important implications for understanding children's cognitive development, problem solving abilities, and academic achievement (Geary, 1995). Geary suggested that cultural factors play an important role in influencing children's perception and cognition. Cultural practices can instill in children a mix of cognitive abilities that may be functional in one social system, but not in others. There is overwhelming evidence that culture plays an important role in children's cognition; different cultures promote different learning styles and problem solving strategies based on their cultural values and backgrounds. However, no study was found to suggest whether culture plays any role in the problem solving of individuals with mental retardation. Nor was there research that supported any particular cognitive strategy as more effective than others in training individuals with mental retardation from different cultural backgrounds to problem solve in social interpersonal situations. It was the purpose of the present study to investigate whether students with mild mental retardation from different cultural backgrounds will problem solve based on their cultural backgrounds. Also, to examine the effects of a general cognitive strategy training based on the general stages of problem solving by D'Zurilla and Goldfried (1971) using interest-based methods of teaching social-interpersonal problem solving skills among African-American students between the ages of 9 and 15 years who have mild mental retardation.

## Cultural Differences

Cultural differences were evident in the students' social problem solving performance. In the spontaneous independent problem solving responses, Nigerian students performed better than Euro-American students and Euro-American students performed better than African-American students (see Table 9). These performance differences are in agreement with Jegede &

Okebukola's (1992) perception of Nigeria as a country. According to them, Nigeria is a predominantly traditional non-western society in which the African mode of thought (often referred to as anthropomorphic) is dominant. In Nigeria, the social and cultural make-up places much value on the extended family and community as part of the immediate family. Children raised in Nigeria may have more opportunity to learn from different sources of how to solve problems, than do children raised in the United States, where the nuclear family may consist of a mother, father and brothers and sisters within that family. Also, Nigerian education presupposes a Nigerian culture, and most students, especially males, are not required to adopt any mode of problem solving that is alien to their culture.

The performance differences between African-Americans and Euro-Americans are in accordance with the bicultural aspect of Anderson's (1988) suggestion that African-American children tend to be at a disadvantage compared to Euro-American students, since they have adopted Euro-American problem solving styles, but perform less well in their utilization. Since American education typically presupposes a Euro-centric culture, African-American students are required to adopt and perform using Euro-centric criteria; however, they generally do not perform at Euro-American standards, perhaps because these modes of social problem solving are alien to their culture.

Cultural differences were also evident in the students' spontaneous social problem solving styles. The independent/non-independent problem solving styles did not significantly vary by cultural grouping (see Table 14) as did the independent problem solving performance (see Table 10). The differences in these findings are the reflection on the two transformed scores used for the problem solving styles. The formulas for the two transformed style scores for problem solving styles, presented earlier in chapter four, looked into the independent responses in relation to non-independent responses across the three cultural groups. However, the independent problem solving performance compared only the independent responses across the three cultural groups. The problem solving styles investigated whether individuals with mild mental retardation from a particular cultural background are more likely than the other to use independent/non-independent problem solving style or individualistic/cooperative problem solving styles when confronted with social interpersonal problem situations. These findings indicated that individuals with mild mental retardation, regardless of their cultural backgrounds, do rely on non-independent problem solving style when faced with social interpersonal problem situations. However, when individualistic/cooperative styles were examined, both American subsamples were significantly more individualistic than the Nigerians. This means that African-American students, overall, appeared to exhibit similar problem solving styles as Euro-American students, who tended to be more individualistic in their problem solving styles. This formula for individualistic/cooperative problem solving styles only looked at the independent responses. The independent problem solving score was the sum of cooperative problem solving and individualistic problem solving scores. Therefore, when the cooperative independent problem solving score was subtracted from the individualistic independent problem solving score, it yielded the individualistic/cooperative problem solving style (see Table 14). These findings are in agreement with the independent problem solving performance (see table 10) findings since both analyses looked into the independent responses.

African-American students appeared to exhibit similar problem solving styles as Euro-American students, however, Euro-American students produced and selected more independent problem solving strategies than did the African-American students. Euro-American children, according to Anderson (1985), move through the educational system where the development of cognitive and learning styles follows a linear, self-reinforcing course. Euro-American children are not asked to be bicultural or bicognitive because the educational system in America is built on the European world view, which tends to benefit them. For African-American children, biculturality is not a free choice, but a prerequisite for successful participation and eventual success. African-American children are expected to be bicultural in order to measure their performance against Euro-American children (Anderson, 1985). Although African-American children may have similar problem solving styles as Euro-Americans, it was the premise of this study for them to learn independent social problem solving methods effectively; they needed to be taught using materials from their own cultural background to improve their performance. For example, Interest-based method proposed using interest-based materials which allows for students' input. This process allows for incorporation and infusion of diverse cultures in the training. The interest-based method is designed to reduce any teaching biases that the trainer may bring into the classroom.

The multiple choice independent problem solving performance did not significantly vary by cultural grouping (see Table 11) and problem solving styles did not vary by cultural grouping (see Table 17) either. This may be due to the fact that there were few error responses in the multiple choice than in spontaneous responses.

In spontaneous responses, participants produced as many as four error responses (other-dependent, avoidance, compliance, and other). However, in the multiple choice responses, students had to choose one out of the four alternatives, two of which were error responses (avoidance and other-dependent).

## Males and Females

Gender differences also played a role in the social problem solving styles: Males performed better on spontaneous independent problem solving responses and spontaneous independent/non-independent problem solving styles. Males were more independent than females, but no significant differences were found between males and females on individualistic social problem solving styles. Similar pattern also existed in the multiple choice responses for both problem solving performance and styles. Males were more independent than females, but no significant differences were found between males and females on individualistic social problem solving styles.

The findings of this study support the observations of TenHouten (1971) in that in social groupings where females are highly subordinated to males, such as Nigeria, females are likely to display less independent modes of problem solving. In a system where they are expected to defer to males, they would be expected to be less independent. In this study, Nigerian females were less likely than Nigerian males to make independent problem solving solutions. Similar pattern of different problem solving style also exists between Euro-American males and females as among the Nigerians. However, among African-Americans, where the status between males and females is more complex and dominance is less determinate, the significant differences in the level of spontaneous independent problem solving styles in the African-Americans tend to be about the same. Though not significant, African-American females tend to be more individualistic independent problem solving styles (see Table 12) than African-American males. In American society, it seems that African-American males are more disadvantaged than African-American females, these results support TenHouten's (1971) theoretical perspective. Barbarin and Soler (1993) suggested in their study that irrespective of age, African-American males are more likely than females to exhibit adjustment difficulties. The sex differences among Euro-American males and females in their problem solving styles support Anderson's (1988) cultural groupings of world views which presented Euro-American males as emphasizing an individualistic approach while most Euro-American females emphasized a group cooperation approach to problem solving.

A trend existed, though not significant (see Tables 8 and 9), in the interactions between culture and sex on the spontaneous responses that indicated more independent problem solving responses for Euro-American and Nigerian males than females. A similar trend existed in the interactions between culture and gender on the spontaneous responses that indicated more individualistic responses (see Table 12) among African-American females compared to males, more independent and individualistic responses for Euro-American and Nigerian males than females.

## Training Effects

In phase II of this study, the students in the interest-based group performed significantly better than those in the traditional group or the control group. These findings are in agreement with Scribner and Cole's (1981) suggestion that the availability of tools (e.g., paper, pencils, crayons) may structure how an individual tends to remember information. The present data indicated that culturally based instruction, based on culturally based materials, created significantly higher posttest results than both the traditional method and the control group and the traditional method generated more independent responses than the control group on social problem solving spontaneous responses and on multiple choice responses. These findings support the argument of Scribner and Cole (1981) that the tools stimulate and shape the cognitive processes that are employed in carrying out an activity. The availability of tools alone without an understanding of their importance and use may not structure how an individual attends and remembers information. These differences suggest that experiences, exposure to material, and understanding of symbolic artifacts are important in any culture to problem solving performance. It is not possible that an individual takes advantage of tools without an understanding of the tools and the skills of literacy. According to Scribner and Cole (1981), the availability of tools and the understanding of how the tools are used, think, is a cultural practice that structures how someone handles cognitive opportunities when they arise. Therefore, African-American children may need to be taught using materials congruent with their own cultural background to improve their performance.

In the Phase 1 of the present study, more African-American males produced avoidance non-independent problem solving responses than Euro-American or Nigerian males. However, in the interest-based group in the phase II of the present study, very few of the African-American males produced avoidance non-independent problem solving responses. They were significantly lower in avoidance than the traditional group and the control group. The data suggest that there is a general tendency among African-American males to produce more than their share of avoidance responses to social problem solving situations, but that culturally appropriate training can dramatically reduce such avoidance.

## Mental Retardation

The findings of this study indicate that students with mild mental retardation learn with the same cultural biases of non-mentally retarded persons. Since they have the mental capacity for communication, although at more rudimentary levels than others who do not have mental retardation, the extent to which they are able to communicate allows them to participate in the culture in which they were raised. These findings support the theoretical argument made by Greenspan, Granfield, and Becker (1991) in their proposed a redefinition of mental retardation as "subaverage intellectual abilities that are reflected in significant deficits in the ability to succeed in roles and activities essential in an individual's primary culture" (p.28).

There is a great need for developing independent problem solving competency among individuals with mental retardation to effectively engage in social interpersonal problem situations they face daily. Knowing that individuals with mild mental retardation are capable of the same cultural biases and disadvantages as those of the same cultural background without mental retardation contributed to our knowledge of how to better educate this population.

## Curriculum Implications

In a multicultural context, it is not practical to design curricula that cater to the cultural backgrounds of all students. It is not efficient to design curricula around the many cultures that exist in each classroom. Therefore, the diversity of the students' cultures become the focal point rather than the curriculum, itself. Often, cultural differences may impact and influence students' ways of functioning in the classroom, and specifically on curricular tasks. An interest-based method allows for the incorporation and infusion of diverse cultures into the curriculum as well as other interest differences based on gender or social class. Interest-based methods can help reduce the Euro-centric bias in the classroom and allow for greater equality of participation on the part of the students. This reduction comes about because students are grouped by interest, which creates its own culture. If, for instance,

Euro-American and African American students differ in cultural backgrounds, they meet on their common ground: love of soccer, and thus lessen the Eurocentric teaching styles in the classrooms. As the pupils experience the interest culture of other students, they learn to embrace the differences in class members through the use of an interest based curriculum.

## Future Research

The next step is to replicate the phase II of this study with Nigerian students to see if the interest-based method of teaching could be beneficial to them, especially the Nigerian females.

**Note:** Every study has limitations, but that does not mean a study is weak. It is a professional practice to state your study's limitations and to recommend future research. This allows your readers to see your credibility.

# REFERENCES

Anderson, J. R. (1985). Cognitive psychology and its implications (2nd ed.). New York: Freeman.

Anderson, J. A. (1988). Cognitive styles and multicultural populations. Journal of Teacher Education, 39, 2-9.

Band, B. E. & Weisz, J. R. (1988). How to feel better when it feels bad: Children=s perspectives on coping with everyday stress. Developmental Psychology, 24, 247-253.

Bates, P. (1980). The effectiveness of interpersonal skills training on the social skill acquisition of moderately and mildly retarded adults. Journal of Applied Behavior Analysis, 13, 237-248.

Bates, P. E., Renzaglia, A., & Clees, T. (1980). Improving the work performance of severely/profoundly retarded young adults: The use of a changing criterion procedural design. Education and Training of the Mentally Retarded, 15, 95-104.

Bellamy, G. T., Inman, D. P., Yeates, J. (1978). Workshop supervision: Evaluation of a procedure for production management with the severely retarded. Mental Retardation, 16, 317-319.

Bregman, S. (1984). Assertiveness training for mentally retarded adults. <u>Mental Retardation, 22,</u> 12-16. Browning, P., & Nave, G. (1993). Teaching social problem solving to learners with mild disabilities. <u>Education and Training in Mental Retardation, 28,</u> 309-317.

Castles, E. E. & Glass, C. R. (1986). Training in social and interpersonal problem-solving skills for mild and moderate mental retarded adults. <u>American Journal of Mental Deficiency, 91,</u> 35-42.

Cole, M. (1989). Cultural psychology: A once and future discipline? <u>Cross-cultural Perspectives, 37,</u> 279-335.

Craighead, L. W., Craighead, W. E., Kazdin, A. E., & Mahoney, M. J. (1994). <u>Cognitive and behavioral interventions: An empirical approach to mental health problems.</u> Allyn and Bacon, Massachusetts.

Cuvo, A. J., Veitch, V. C., Trace, M. W., & Konke, J. L. (1978). Teaching change computation to the mentally retarded. <u>Behavior Modification, 2,</u> 531-548.

Dolman, D., & Williamson, J. (1983). <u>Teaching problem solving strategies.</u> Menlo Park: Addison Wesley.

D'Zurilla, T. J. & Goldfried, M. R. (1971). Problem solving and behavior modification. <u>Journal of Abnormal Psychology, 78,</u> 107-126.

Foxx, R. M., McMorrow, M. J., & Schloss, C. N. (1983). Stacking the deck: Teaching social skills to retarded adults with a modified table game. Journal of Applied Behavior Analysis, 16, 157-170.

Geary, D. C. (1995). Reflections of evolution and culture in children's cognition: Implications for mathematical development and instruction. American Psychological Association, 50, 24-37.

Gelman, R. (1993). A rational-constructivist account of early learning about numbers and objects. In D. L. Medin (Ed.), The psychology of learning and motivation: Advances in research and theory, 30, 61-96. San Diego, CA: Academic Press.

Gold, M. W. (1972). Stimulus factors in skill training of retarded adolescents on a complex assembly task: Acquisition, transfer, and retention. American Journal of Mental Deficiency, 76, 517-526.

Gold, M. W. (1976). Task analysis of a complex assembly task by the retarded blind. Exceptional Children, 43, 78-84.

Goldstein, K. M., & Blackman, S. (1978). Cognitive style: Five approaches and relevant research. New York: John Wiley & Sons.

Greenspan, S. (1979). Social intelligence in the retarded. In N. R. Ellis (Ed.). Handbook of mental deficiency: Psychological theory and research (2nd ed.), 483-531. Hillsdale, NJ. Erlbaum.

Hensen, M., & Eisler, R. M. (1976). Social skills training. In W. E. Craighead, A. E. Kazdin, & M. J. Mahoney (Eds.), Behavior Modification: Principles, issues, and applications, 361-375. Boston : Houghton-Mifflin.

Jegede, O. J., & Okebukola, P. A. (1992). Differences in sociocultural environment perceptions associated with gender in science classrooms. Journal of Research in Science Teaching, 29, 637-647.

Kaufman, R. (1979). Identifying and solving problems: A system approach (2nd ed.). La Jolla, CA: University Association.

Keogh, D. A., Faw, G. D., Whitman, T. L., & Reid, D. H. (1984). Enhancing leisure skills in severely retarded adolescents through a self-instructional treatment package. Analysis and Intervention in Developmental Disabilities, 4, 333-351.

Martin, G., Pallotta-Cornick, A., Johnstone, G., & Goyos, A. C. (1980). A supervisory strategy to improve work performance for lower functioning retarded clients in a sheltered workshop. Journal of Applied Behavioral Analysis, 13, 183-190.

McDonnell, J. J., & Ferguson, B. (1988). A comparison of general case in vivo and general case stimulation plus in vivo training. Journal of the Association for Persons with Severe Handicaps, 13,116-124.

Naisbitt, J. (1982). Megatrends. New York: Warner Books.

Page, T. J., Iwata, B. A., & Neef, N. A. (1976). Teaching pedestrian skills to retarded persons: Generalization from the classroom to the natural environment. Journal of Applied Behavior Analysis, 9, 433-444.

Risley, T. R., & Cuvo, A. (1980). Training mentally retarded adults to make emergence telephone calls. Behavior Modification, 4, 513-526.

Scribner, S., & Cole, M. (1981). The psychology of literacy. Cambridge, MA: Harvard University Press.

Senatore, V., Matson, J. L., & Kazdin, A. E. (1982). A comparison of behavioral methods to train social skills to mentally retarded adults. Behavior Therapy, 13, 313-324.

Shade, B. J., & Edwards, P. A. (1987). Ecological correlates of the educative style of Afro-American children. Journal of Negro Education, 56, 88-99.

Spivack, G., Platt, J. J., & Shure, M. B. (1976). The problem-solving approach to adjustment. San Francisco. Jossey-Bass.

Stacy, D., Doleys, D. M., Malcolm, R. (1979). Effects of social-skills training in a community-based program. <u>American Journal of Mental Deficiency, 84,</u> 152-158.

Strain, P. (1975). Increasing social play of severely retarded preschoolers through sociodramatic activities. <u>Mental Retardation, 13,</u> 7-9.

TenHouten, W. D. (1971). <u>Cognitive styles and the social order.</u> Final Report, part II, OEO Study B00-5135, Thought, race, and opportunity. Los Angeles, CA: University of California, Los Angeles.

Treffinger, D., Speedie, S., & Brunner, W. (1974). Improving children's creative problem solving ability: The prude creativity project. <u>Journal of Creative Behavior, 8,</u> 20-30.

Wehman, P., & Marchant, J. A. (1978). Improving free play skills of severely retarded children. <u>The American Journal of Occupational Therapy, 32,</u> 100-104.

Zigler, E. (1969). Development vs. difference theories of mental retardation and the problem motivation. <u>American Journal of Mental Deficiency, 73,</u> 536-556.